It Happened in Dedham:

THE BLACK CAT STRIKES OAKDALE

**Peggy O'Connell O'Neill
and Mary Parker**

THE BLACK CAT STRIKES OAKDALE

This book is about a close-knit neighborhood in a section of Dedham Massachusetts called Oakdale. It is a true tale of how children find help from adults to navigate through a problem that arises. Learning to trust adults and see how other kids accept you as you are, well, that is just the greatest thing!

Peg and Peanuts
M. F.

<u>*ACKNOWLEDGEMENTS*</u>

I would like to take this time to thank the very special kids (now adults) in the neighborhood who, without them, there wouldn't have been the true story of "<u>The</u> <u>Black Cat Strikes Oakdale!!</u>" With their Real Names: Ellen Sherbs, Karen Sherbs, Janet Sherbs, Ellen Carty, MaryAnn Carty, Johnny Carty, Peter Carty, Steven Carty, Kathleen, and Mary-Clare Sullivan, LeAnn McComb Tibets, Susan Cahoon, Eddie Pierce,

Marion Harding, my mother Mary, my father Tom, as well as my sisters; Amy and Karen.

You are all vital to this story and I cannot express enough gratitude to you for being in my life and tolerating my "bossiness"! Ha, Ha!

I also want to express my gratitude and make a special mention of my husband Walter O'Neill and my sister Amy MacMannis- Freeland. My husband acted as my consultant on many decisions I had to make for this book. He handled it with a <u>LOT</u> of patience and stopped everything to help.

He was also my cheering coach when I felt downhearted!

My sister Amy was instrumental in getting this book from manuscript to publishing which was a big challenge for me. I don't know what I would have done without her advice and counseling throughout this process.

Thank you, Thank you, to all the aforementioned, for all your extremely valuable contributions!!

DEDICATION

I would also like to dedicate this book to my beloved sister Karen. This trip down memory lane meant so much more with her in it. She was a loving wife to her husband Ed Loftus and a devoted mother to three children: Alice, Robert, and John. Karen was also a doting grandmother to five grandchildren whom she enjoyed immensely.

Karen's passing left a hole in the

hearts of my family that will never be filled, except for the many fond memories we have of her. She is sorely missed. I know she would love the books we have written about the childhood we shared and the many friends we had/have in the neighbor-hood of Oakdale.

<u>We love you, Karen</u>.

Table of Contents

<u>INTRODUCTION</u>

I am going to tell you a story that happened in Oakdale, a neighborhood in Dedham, Mass. We were just moving into a home right across the street from the Oakdale Elementary School! This was going to be great!

The Elementary school was a really nice-looking building. It was all brick and stone and had this round entryway surrounding the big wooden front doors.

If you went around the back, there was a big courtyard with back doors that led to the classrooms for all the grades. That is where we would have recess every day!

I was six, soon to be seven and was starting second grade! I was nervous but mostly excited to go to public school. It had to be better than my old school in Franklin, Mass. The teachers were nuns and they hit us with rulers on our hands if we were bad! Really, they did!!

Take a step back into the 1960's like you are in a dream... as my Mom, Karen, my baby sister Amy, and I enter our house for the first time on 130 Cedar Street in Dedham, Mass.

CHAPTER ONE

The New House

I remember the day we walked into the kitchen at 130 Cedar Street, Dedham Massachusetts. We were moving into an area of the town called Oakdale. Cedar Street was quite a busy street since it connected to one of the major highways in the town. All the houses that were in our neighborhood were on one side of the street, I noticed. They were two story homes, mainly.

And the *WHOLE* other side of the Street was the Oakdale School. It took up most of the block! <u>AND</u> our house was right across the street next to the crosswalk. How great was that??

Karen and I went inside the house and ran around to look at all the rooms. The kitchen was really old-fashioned. The sink was way across the room from the refrigerator, and the stove on the other wall! Crazy! (We would redo the whole kitchen eventually.)

There was a staircase from there that had very steep stairs and led to Karen's and my bedroom. Someone was always

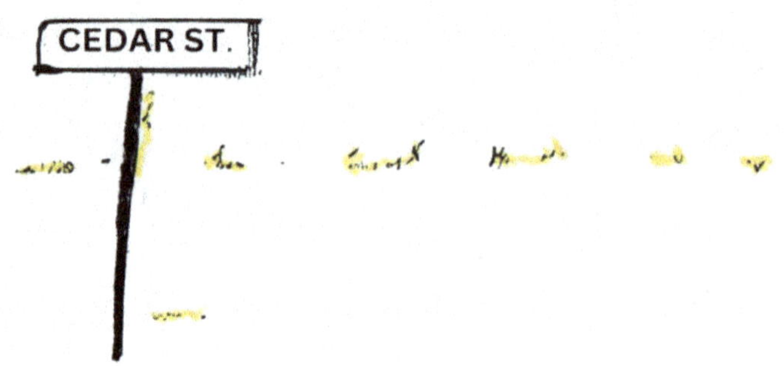

falling down those last few stairs!

It was a really big bedroom with

windows all down one wall. You could

look out onto the neighbor's house and yard, plus the sidewalk. My gosh! This was going to be fun!

From the kitchen we could walk through the big dining room, and we would be in the living room at the front of the house. This would be the perfect place for the piano. My Mom played the piano and sang all the time, so now we could hear her all through the house!

My Mom was holding my baby sister, Amy, in her arms and feeding her a bottle in the kitchen. There was a back door off there that led to a huge porch. The next thing you know a woman was at the door. It turns out she was the mom who lived next door. She came over to meet us!

I would later find out that her name was Mrs. Stack. She looked a lot different than my Mom did. She wore simpler clothing, and her hair was gray, so she was older looking. My Mom told me soon after she left, that she had eight kids. No wonder she had gray hair!

Mrs. Stack was very nice. I thought it was great that there were so many kids right next door! We surely would have kids to play with. Karen and I were so excited!

Mrs. Stack told us about her kids, especially the ones she thought we could play with. The three youngest of the children were girls, thankfully!

The oldest was Janet, who was one year older than me. The middle of the three was Ellen. She was in between Karen's and my age. The youngest was Karen; yes, another Karen, and she was a year younger than my sister Karen. So, for the rest of the story, so there is no confusion, we will call our neighbor, Karen S.

We did not meet the kids that day,

since we were not moving in yet. My Dad still had to sign some papers and then we would have a moving truck move all our stuff in.

It seemed like forever but, finally moving day came about a week later. A lot of the kids from the neighborhood came to meet us; the girls from next door, Patsy Carey, Kathleen, and Mary-Clare Gallivan!

Since I was shy, my Mom stepped up and said, "Well, hello there kids," kind of loudly, "It's so nice of you to come and meet us on our special moving day! What are your names?" (The moving truck and guys were very loud!)

They each told us their names, which would take us a while to remember, for sure! Karen and I said, "Hi", kind of quietly, and then we had to go sort out the boxes with my Mom.

She said, "O.K.., kids, we have to go inside now, but maybe the girls can come out to play later." My Mom was getting tired of holding Amy and you could tell the kids were **very interested** in baby Amy. Later, they could meet her in her playpen.

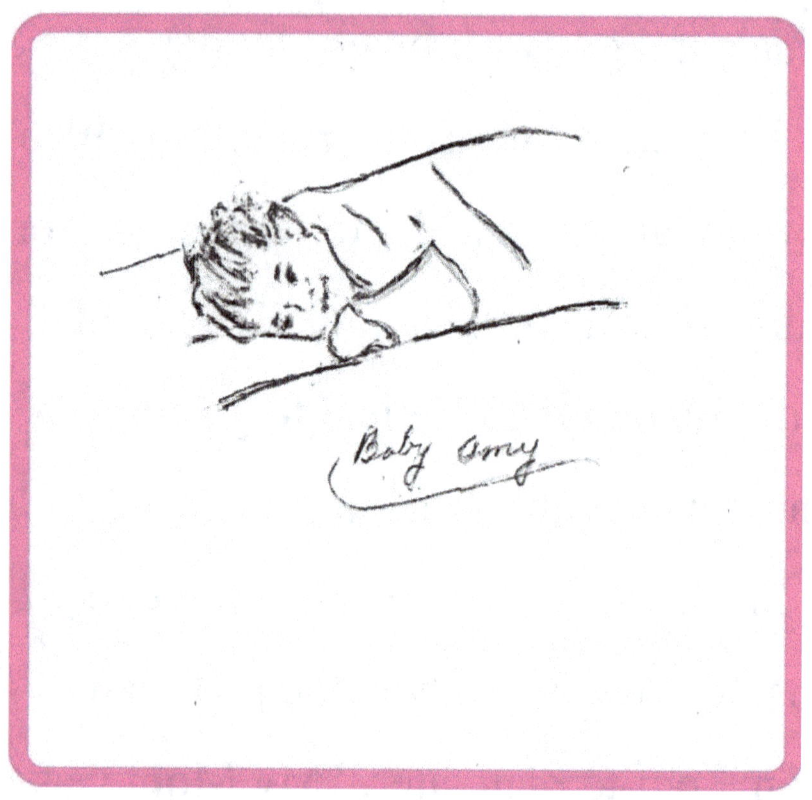

So, as far as who we played with, it turns out that we hung out with Karen S. and Ellen the most. Janet would hang out with me sometimes and I called her my best friend. But she was moody and at times had no patience with me at all, yeah...maybe because I was a year younger, I don't know...

All three girls had blond hair of different colors. They had blue eyes, too. Ellen had the blondest hair and was about the same size as me, even though she was a year or so younger. Ellen was over our house the most of all, really!

She was quite easy to get along with and was happy most of the time. Karen S. hung out with us, too, but since she was younger than me, she played with my sister Karen.

She had a little darker blond hair. We used to call it "dirty blond" back then, even though it was not dirty!! Wacky, right?

Karen S. was what my Mom called "accident-prone." Yeah, she fell off her

bike a lot and skinned her knees. We

had to keep a big supply of band-aids handy! Haha! Really, we liked each other a lot and enjoyed playing as a group, too!

Moving down the street was the Carey family. Una and Pat Carey were from Ireland. I was fascinated by their accent and their customs. They lived right next door to the Stack's house. They had six kids: three girls and three boys. Karen and I were so lucky because the three girls were close to our age, just like the Stack's girls.

Ellen and MaryAnn Carey were twins but looked nothing alike and Patsy was the youngest. She played with my sister Amy when they were toddlers. We were always trying to stay away from the boys because they would aggravate us sometimes (Boys did that to girls all the time...).

Ellen had pretty, reddish-brown hair and it was long and thick. Her eyes were like the color of her hair. She wore her hair in braids a lot and she had a lot of freckles all over her skin. Her sister MaryAnn had long blond hair, and she might have had blue eyes. I can't remember, exactly.

MaryAnn had freckles, too. They

were lighter colored and not as many as Ellen, I would say. Now you know why I said they looked nothing alike, right? Patsy had darker hair and freckles sprinkled across her nose. She looked a lot like her mom, Una (I thought so, anyhow).

They were taller and bigger girls than we were. Their Mom and Dad were tall, too, and so were the boys. We got along well with the girls, and they played with us when they were allowed to go down the street.

The last house on our end of the street was where the Gallivan family lived.

They were a small family, like ours, and there were four kids. Timmy was the oldest, Kathleen was next in line, then Johnny, and Mary- Clare was the youngest.

Of course, we did not want to hang out with Timmy and Johnny, their being boys and all, but sometimes when we played group games, we would let them join in.

Kathleen played with my sister Karen and I. Mary-Clare would become best friends with my sister Amy, as they got older. Kathleen was kind of a nervous kid, but we sort of ignored that. She had long strawberry blond hair and a freckled face. She was a good kid and joined in all the games down our end of the street.

We also played with LeAnn Combs. She was a little girl that Mrs. Stack watched during the day while LeAnn's Mom went to work. She was a little shy at first but played with whoever was outside really.

LeAnn was petite and had blondish hair. We considered her a part of everything that happened in the neighborhood because she was there all the time!! Yup, that's the way it worked in our neighborhood. Especially if you were a *GIRL*!!

Here is some stuff about the Cedar Street kids: Most of the time, we were all good kids cause parents were strict in those days.

Side note: Some parents were stricter than others and some kids might actually "get the switch," if they did something wrong. We called it a "spanking".

A switch was a twig you would pick off a tree or a bush and take all the leaves off. A couple of pats on the backside and that was the punishment.

Whoa...my sister Karen and I would stay away from those houses for a couple of days until things calmed down. Sheesh...

My Mom and Dad were a bit younger so they would use the Dr. Spock book for fixing kid's problems. That was o.k. because we were good most of the time! Right, right!

CHAPTER TWO

A New Member of the Family

It was a few years later that we got a kitten. My parents wanted Karen and I to be old enough to take care of the kitten, so they waited until I was about 9 years old, and Karen was seven. My Dad said we would have to feed the kitten and clean out the litter box, yeah...yuck!

Our Uncle Tommy brought this really, really, cute kitten with him one day and we loved it right away! He said his neighbor's cat had kittens and was trying to find homes for them. He called and asked my Mom and Dad if it was o.k. that we took one. ***AND THEY SAID YES!***

The kitten had big white paws and was striped with brown and white. The brown was like the color of peanut butter. He was sooo...soft! Amy yelled out, ***"WE SHOULD CALL HIM PEANUTS! HE LOOKS LIKE THE***

COLOR OF PEANUT BUTTER, *ha-ha!"* she laughed! Karen and I thought for once, Amy had a great idea, so we agreed and that was it! "Ok, Ame, from now on, we will call him Peanuts! Ha-Ha!" I chuckled. "Yeah, we will call him Peanuts, Ha-Ha!" Karen joined in.

We were all laughing at this point. Ya know how one when person starts laughing hysterically and you start laughing too, and you cannot stop, and you don't know even why you started laughing in the first place? Well, that's what happened!

I don't know why we all found it so funny. Eesh, I guess it was because it was Amy's idea! She being the youngest and all, we didn't expect her to have such a good idea!

Peanuts was a very smart kitten and was growing into the ***BEST KITTEN EVER!!*** We had to train Peanuts to use the litter box and set up a place for him to sleep. He was very smart and learned everything really fast! We made a comfy bed with blankets in the back entryway to the house. Peanuts loved it there because it was so cozy!

All the kids in the neighborhood loved Peanuts because he was such a lovable kitten! We used to take him out in a doll carriage and walk him around the neighborhood like he was a baby! Peanuts even let us put doll clothes on him and a hat that had cat ears. I do not even know where we got that hat, but he still let us put it on him. Peanuts *really*

was incredible!

Oh....I remember now. That Cat Hat was Amy's hat that she wore when she was a baby!Ha-ha!

My Nana from Franklin knitted a baby sweater and that hat for Amy! Nana was an expert knitter, for sure! She would knit us hats and mittens every year to wear, just in time for the winter.

I really looked forward to seeing what colors she picked and trying on the hat and mittens that seemed to always fit so perfectly. No matter how much we grew every year, they were always just right!!! They were nice and warm, and Amy wore them all the time.

She really didn't mind wearing that hat but when the school crossing guard would tweak the ears on it, my Mom would whisper, "Please, God, don't let Amy cry." and make the sign of the cross on her chest. Nobody wanted to hear Amy cry because she was *VERY, VERY LOUD* and it seemed like she would never stop!

So, my Mom would say a quick prayer! Ha-ha! I thought that was so funny, I don't know why! Right here I am going to tell you *my* version of what happened next, and then I will tell you my Mom's version.

CHAPTER THREE

The BLACK CAT Arrives

It was a nice, bright summer morning that Karen and I woke up to. We didn't have to start school yet, so we had the whole summer to look forward to! We wanted to get out and see who was around to play with.

After breakfast, we walked up the

street to see if there was anything going on with the Stack's kids, but it was quiet. I said to Karen, "They are probably still doing their chores, so let's see if the Carey kids are out." With so many kids in the house, Mrs. Stack kept the family busy helping with chores every day.

Karen agreed, so we continued to walk further and came to the entrance of the Carey's driveway and back door. We started to get closer and saw that there was a bit of commotion with the boys.

We made our way down to see Johnny

and Peter dancing around this sleek, all black, shiny cat with slanted green eyes. MaryAnn and Ellen C. were yelling at them to stop.

The cat was **HUGE!** I never saw any other cat look like him before! Not in our neighborhood, anyways! This cat had black shiny fur all over and I think a little white patch near his mouth. If you got closer, he would spit and growl at you, so *FORGET ABOUT IT!* He would not be anyone's pet. He just stared at us with a look that made chills run up my back!

So, this cat was bad news! I said

loudly, *"YOU GUYS YOU CAN'T FEED HIM BECAUSE HE WILL KEEP COMING BACK AND YOU WILL HAVE TO KEEP HIM AND TAKE CARE OF HIM AND YOUR MOM AND DAD WON'T LET YOU KEEP HIM, I KNOW IT!"* I was quite annoyed with them because they looked at me like I was weird. Karen yelled, *"YEAH, HE WILL KEEP COMING BACK!"* She thought I was right about most things.

We thought it was a bad situation, this cat, and I thought the Carey kids seemed to be enjoying the whole deal.

Ellen Carey said, "Don't worry! I will make sure they do not feed the BLACK CAT, Peggy." Since she was the oldest, she was the boss of her brothers and sisters, which was good!

So, we left, and continued up the sidewalk to check if the Gallivan's were outside. We called for them, *"HI-OH KATHLEEN, COME OUT AND PLAY!"* and she came running out of the house as we all headed back towards our house.

By the way, we called for all the kids in the neighborhood like that. The Stack's girls told us when we first moved in. You yelled *Hi-Oh!* First and then the kids' names you wanted to play with. Sometimes we would add,

"COME OUT AND PLAY!", too.

It depended on if we had already called for them once already on that day.

We ignored the Carey kids while we told Kathleen the whole story about the BLACK CAT. She agreed with Karen and I that this was not going to be a good thing. "He seems scary looking, doesn't he?", Kathleen said. "The Carey kids have been feeding him for a couple of days, I think." she whispered. I said, "Oh Jeez, that is not good at all. That BLACK CAT is going to keep coming back, now."

By now the Stack's kids were out and we all told them about the BLACK CAT. It was now getting to be the talk of the neighborhood!! What was to become of this BLACK CAT? Was he going to stay with the Carey's? Was he going to leave and never come back, and this was just a one-time thing?

We discussed each of these ideas before we got bored and went off to play. Later on, we all had to go home for dinner. We had a long day of playing Hide and Seek, Red Light, Freeze Tag, and other games. Karen and I sat and told our Mom and Dad about the BLACK CAT situation at the Carey's house.

Usually, our parents would humor us, and act extremely interested in our daily stories. I could tell they really enjoyed our excitement but, this time it was different. My Dad was asking us a lot of questions about this BLACK CAT. He asked, "Where did you see this BLACK CAT?" and "When did this BLACK CAT show up? How long was he at the Carey's house? Do you kids know? You said they were feeding the cat??"

As my Mom listened carefully, Karen and I took turns answering the questions. Amy laughed out loud at our telling of the story. Since she was a toddler at this point, she really did not understand what we were talking about anyway. I got really mad at her though and yelled, ***"AME, CUT IT OUT! THIS IS NOT FUNNY! THIS IS NOT A GOOD THING. THIS BLACK CAT WAS MEAN TO US!"***, and then I got yelled at by my Mom for yelling at her. Sheesh!

I was doing all the answering of my Dad's questions, while Karen would jump in, repeating me, as usual. I told him, "I don't know a lot, Dad, but the

BLACK CAT was there this morning. That's when we saw it. And yes. The Carey kids were feeding it."

My Dad said, "I don't know why, but I have a bad feeling about this BLACK CAT too, kids. We will just have to keep our eyes open as to where this cat shows up again. And, we will have to keep our Peanuts away from him. I am *counting* on you and Karen to keep a close eye on Peanuts from now on."

Dinner was now over so Karen and I washed and dried the dishes. I swept the kitchen floor and then it was bath time. Back then, we took baths together in the downstairs bathroom about once a week. We were not that poor, but we always had to "pinch our pennies" as people said back then. It just meant we all had to be a bit careful about how much heat, electricity, and water we used every day.

It wasn't like we thought about it. It was common at that time, in our neighborhood, for sisters to take baths together. Sooo...once we finished bathing, we went off to bed.

CHAPTER FOUR

The BLACK CAT Attack

You have not heard me mention much about Peanuts for a while because he really became a part of everything we did! He might tag along and go from one yard to the next or he would lay in the sun on the back porch of our house. Peanuts liked looking at everything that was going on in the neighborhood so he would sit on a windowsill, inside the house. If he was thirsty, he had figured out that he could walk along the side edge of the bathtub downstairs. Then, he would jump up on his hind paws to the edge of the sink, right next to the tub.

Peanuts would tap the faucet with one paw and get it to drip so he could get a drink! ***ARE YOU KIDDING ME??*** Seriously, Peanuts really was a VERY, VERY smart kitten! The whole family and the neighborhood really loved him.

Back at our yard, all of us kids were talking and wondering if the BLACK CAT had taken off. Was he getting fed at someone else's house? We wondered, because we had not seen him around in the neighborhood.

Ellen S. yelled, *"WELL, GOOD RIDDANCE TO THE MEAN BLACK CAT!"* And I yelled, *"YEAH, I HOPE HE NEVER COMES BACK!"* While Karen chimed in, *"YEAH, I HOPE HE NEVER COMES BACK!"* She always did that, repeated what I said. It annoyed me, but most of the time, I did not want to take the time to argue with her about knocking that off!

It was time for a snack, so we all headed to each of our houses to get something to eat. As Karen and I came around the corner to our back walkway,

we saw the BLACK CAT!

"WHAAAATT???" We both started

screaming out loud.

The BLACK CAT was fighting with Peanuts who was not really fighting back! We yelled and jumped up and down at the ***BLACK CAT, "GET OFF PEANUTS! STOP IT! GET AWAY!!"*** and it was amazing, but he ran off!

Peanuts had a couple of cuts around his face and on his paw, so we carried him up the back stairs. We told our Mom what happened right away. She was on the phone with her best friend Kay who she talked to every day!!

She quickly hung up the phone when she saw how upset we were, and she noticed Peanuts was bleeding. The three of us took turns wiping off the blood and checking the scratches.

I asked my Mom rather loudly, "Ma, why didn't Peanuts fight back? I don't get it! He just stood there while the BLACK CAT made awful growling and screaming noises! He kept punching his paws onto Peanuts with his nails out and Peanuts didn't do anything!".

My Mom asked "Well, how long were you two standing there?" Then she said "Peanuts didn't fight back because he is a good, nice cat. He has never had to fight, so he really didn't know what to do, since this has never happened to him before."

Well, that seemed like a reasonable explanation to us. Then I answered, "Ma, it was only a couple of seconds before we yelled at the BLACK CAT to get off Peanuts. And then Ellen S. cried, ***"YEAH, WE REALLY YELLED AT THE BLACK CAT, LOUD!"*** I was so upset, I hadn't even noticed that Ellen S. was trailing right behind us.

Now, I will tell you my mom's version of what happened to Peanuts: She said it was just a "Ho-hum" day. It seemed like things had really calmed down a bit on Cedar Street since the kids were on school vacation. No more ironing and following schedules!!

My Mom was trying to relax when suddenly she heard high pitched screaming; she said it sounded like girls screaming! "Where is it coming from??", she wondered. It sounded like it was coming from the back porch!

She thought it might be the kids or animals screaming. *IT WAS BOTH!!* (Mothers are always trying to imagine a scene before they get there. I know that's impossible, but that's what they do.) Mom went racing to the back door. Out near the cat dish, she could see

Peanuts being attacked by this *HUGE BLACK CAT!* (I know, I know, I am exaggerating a little. But it was really BIG!)

Let's remember that our beautiful, yellow striped Peanuts, was still a kitten. Mom yelled, *"RUN, PEANUTS, RUN!"* but she could not get there fast enough. She grabbed a broom from the back doorway and began pushing the BLACK CAT away from our poor, brave little victim.

Peanuts was just a house cat who had never been far beyond our back door. He never killed a mouse or a bird; he just wanted to play with us kids.

Next, thing you know, I was running to help. All the other kids followed me; my Karen, Karen S., Ellen, and Sue (she lived on the street behind ours). They were yelling in a loud, frightening chorus, ***"RUN, PEANUTS, RUN!"***

Our poor yellow cat ran his bruised and battered body back to us where we stood! Somehow, in that moment, we all thought Peanuts looked prouder than usual. He didn't win the fight, but he stuck it out until he couldn't take anymore!"

Just then, my Dad came home, and we

were all very excited as we told him about what had happened to Peanuts. He was mad when he heard about it and spoke loudly "I *KNEW* when you told us about that cat that he was going to be bad news, but I never thought *THIS* could happen!"

We had set Peanuts down to rest and lie down inside the house. We could watch him more closely if he was *in* the house and away from the stupid BLACK CAT! (I know it's bad to say the word stupid, but I was really upset!) Then we headed out to tell the neighborhood kids what happened.

After dinner, the Stack's kids came over and said they wanted to see Peanuts, but I said, "We have to keep him safe from that BLACK CAT because he hates Peanuts and acts like he wants to kill him! We need to tell the Carey kids to stop feeding him and about what happened. <u>AND</u> tell the Gallivan's too. Everyone needs to watch out for the BLACK CAT ever coming near Peanuts *again*!"

CHAPTER FIVE

The BLACK CAT Returns

As you can tell, we kids were on a MISSION! The Stack's and Karen and I thought I was the boss of the whole mission. My bossiness came in very handy this time! I mean, Peanuts was *our* cat after all, and I was the oldest kid sooo....

We got to the Carey kids house, and they were in the driveway hanging around on bikes. Ellen S. piped up this time and told them what happened to Peanuts. She yelled, *"YOU BETTER STOP FEEDING THAT MEAN BLACK CAT!!"* to the group. Johnny Carey, the oldest of the boys yelled back, *"WE CAN DO ANYTHING WE WANT; YOU AREN'T THE BOSS OF US!!"*

Right then, we knew the boys were still feeding the BLACK CAT! At that, I could feel my heart starting to pound and my face getting red, and I yelled,

"YOU STUPID HEAD, JOHNNY CAREY, DON'T YOU GET IT? THAT BLACK CAT TRIED TO KILL PEANUTS AND IF YOU KEEP FEEDING HIM, HE WILL KEEP COMING BACK AND TRY TO KILL PEANUTS AGAIN AND IT WILL BE ALL YOUR FAULT!'?" as I gasped for a breath. (I know. I called him a bad name and I lost my temper. I was sorry for it later. If my Mom and Dad knew, I would get yelled at for sure!)

Then Ellen Carey told him to shush up and said that they would never feed him again. Well, she did say that **before**, but this time it sounded like she *really* meant it. Whatever Ellen said ruled. We felt sure that this would be the end of them feeding the BLACK CAT.

So, some time passed, and we all figured he must have been being fed somewhere else because he disappeared for *so* long. One day Ellen S. whispered to Karen and me, "That BLACK CAT hasn't been around for a while, so maybe it's safe for Peanuts to play outside again with us?" and I said, "Hey, yeah, you know, you're right. I'll ask my Mom if Peanuts can go outside now."

That night at dinner I asked my Mom and Dad if they thought it was safe enough for Peanuts to start going outside more and start playing with us in the neighborhood. They agreed that it would be fine, so we took Peanuts out for a spin in the baby carriage and all the kids came over to say, "**Hi!**" They really missed seeing Peanuts and took turns patting him on his head and paws.

Wouldn't you know, now that we finally felt safe letting Peanuts out; Karen was running from the Stack's back yard about a week or so later. She said, "Peggy, I swear, I just saw the

BLACK CAT creeping around Eddie Pearson's yard. I have to tell Dad!"

Right behind our back yard was Eddie Pearson's yard.

His sister Marion owned the house. That's where we played all our games with the other neighborhood kids because Marion said it was ok. It was the perfect place for us to play! There were two huge trees at each end of the yard that were exactly right for us to play Hide and Seek, Red Light, Freeze Tag, and Giant Step.

Sometimes, out of the blue, Marion would invite Karen and me in and give us a glass of milk and a cookie. We LOVED that! She would work around the kitchen and be cleaning and chatting with us. Marion was an old person too, but she got around very well and was still working, I think. We were so lucky, weren't we?

O.k., so back to the BLACK CAT sighting. I told Karen to tell our Dad when he got home from work, and we were eating dinner. Karen said, "Yeah, that's a good idea. We have to talk about getting a plan ready."

Soon enough, Dad came home, and we were all sitting around the dinner table. When my Dad finished talking to my Mom, I gave Karen a little nudge and she piped up and said excitedly,

"Dad, guess what? I saw the BLACK CAT coming around today. He was coming out of Eddie Pearson's yard! Then when he saw me, he ran off. But for sure, he is back in the neighborhood."

My Dad said, "This BLACK CAT has it in for Peanuts and it is clear he won't stop until he *KILLS* him." he said loudly. I could see he was trying to stay calm even though his cheeks were turning pink! "So, after dinner, let's go out on the porch and I will tell you what we are going to do," he continued.

Karen and I rushed through cleaning

the dishes and sweeping the floor and ran out onto the porch where my Dad was waiting.

<u>The Meeting</u>

CHAPTER SIX

The PLAN

We sat at the picnic table and my Dad said, "Ok, I am going to need you both to help me with **THIS PLAN**, so here is what I am thinking. The BLACK CAT most likely will come through the back yard so Peggy, you will dangle a can of tuna a few inches from the ground from the top of the porch. I will wrap a piece of rope around it, so it will not come undone.

Then Karen, you are going to be on the lookout. You will always have to be looking for the BLACK CAT showing up in our back yard." Karen said, "O.K. Dad. I know what I have to do."

My Dad continued, "When the BLACK CAT shows up near our back yard, I will get a trash can ready and lay it down on the ground. Then when Peggy dangles the tuna in front of the BLACK CAT, I will scoop the BLACK CAT into the trash can and put it into the trunk of the car. We can all take the BLACK CAT over to Canton and leave him in a nice neighborhood where he will get fed." (Canton was about two towns away).

We all nodded, and my Dad said to my Mom, "Mary, this is the best way, I think, to move the BLACK CAT far enough away so he can't hurt Peanuts. I can't imagine he could find his way back from Canton to Oakdale, do you?"

Mom answered, "This **PLAN** is a really clever idea if everyone does their part. Hopefully, we will never see that BLACK CAT again. I like that he will be in a nice neighborhood too. People are sure to take care of him in Canton."

And so, we waited for the day we would try to capture the BLACK CAT. We all knew **THE PLAN**; what each of us was supposed to do. It was just a matter of time before we were to put **THE PLAN** into action.

You might be wondering why we just didn't take the BLACK CAT to a local animal shelter. Well, my Dad told us that it wouldn't be fair to give this cat to anyone else because he was so bad and so mean. So that is why we had to do this. <u>And,</u> the shelters put animals to sleep if they aren't taken after a few days. (They did that back then, but nowadays they don't).

"The cat will be fine", he said. "He has survived off the streets for a long time and he will be able to fend for himself, now. Just like he did when he arrived at the Carey kids' house. Someone will feed him." he reassured us.

Weeks went by and the summer was getting hotter, so we put box fans in the bedroom windows. We tried to stay cool under the shade of the trees outside during the day as we played till dark, and the streetlights came on. It was GREAT!

I could hear cats fight outside sometimes at night but, we always made sure that Peanuts was locked inside the breezeway out back so he would be safe. And then it happened!

We were playing in the Stack's yard and spotted the BLACK CAT slinking around their trash cans, looking for something to eat!! Ellen and Karen S. were there and my sister, too. I grabbed Karen's arm and screamed at the top of my lungs, *"IS THAT THE BLACK CAT THAT TRIED TO KILL*

PEANUTS? AM, I DREAMING?" as I pointed towards the BLACK CAT with my mouth hanging open. Everyone looked at each other, you know, like we all knew what to do. We very quietly started creeping towards the Black Cat.

Suddenly he turned his head and looked straight at us as we screamed, *"THAT'S HIM, THAT'S REALLY HIM!"* Then the BLACK CAT ran off!

We all started running like mad back to our yard and then finally stopped breathless as we sat on the swings and the grass. I panted and said to Ellen and Karen S., "I think it was really him because he had those slanted green eyes like before." Then Ellen said "Yeah, for sure that was him. It looked exactly like him, but how is it possible? It's been so long since he has been around!" We sat there shaking our heads.

Then Ellen asked, "Are you going to tell your Mom and Dad?" And I said, as I looked toward our Karen, "Yes, for sure we will tell our Mom and Dad at dinner in a little while. We have to figure out what to do about this BLACK CAT because if he came back to try and kill Peanuts, he has another thing coming!!"

My Mom called us in for dinner a few minutes later so the kids ran over to their house as we ran inside. As we all settled down for dinner, I waited for the best moment to pipe into my Mom and Dad's discussion. My Dad had a rule that we should never interrupt him and my Mom at the dinner table.

Finally, there was a pause and I said "Mom, Dad, we really need to tell you something!"And just as I was about to get into full swing with all the details, Karen yells, *"THE BLACK CAT IS BACK!!"* I squeezed her arm and got yelled at for it, but she messed up my whole story!

Anyway, I told them that the BLACK CAT was back. "No lie, I bet you don't believe us, but you can see for yourself, because he is creeping around everyone's trash in the neighborhood. That BLACK CAT looked at all of us kids and stared with those ugly green eyes. ***THAT'S HOW WE KNOW IT'S HIM!"*** I spoke a bit louder than usual.

"Boy, that cat; he really has a vendetta against Peanuts, (that means The BLACK CAT had a plan that was ***no good***), and then my Dad said, "Karen, Peggy, remember **THE PLAN** I told you about a couple of weeks ago? It's time..."

CHAPTER SEVEN

The BLACK CAT Capture

Karen and I went out to play and thankfully the kids were already outside. Ellen asked us what our parents said about the whole BLACK CAT situation. I told them my Dad had a **PLAN** and told them every detail. We all nodded our heads in agreement because we all thought it was a good **PLAN.**

We ran off and played until the streetlights came on and then went home. We all knew it was only a matter of time before the BLACK CAT would come strolling through *our* yard. Sure enough, I swear it was only a couple of days when Karen spotted the *BLACK CAT IN OUR OWN BACK YARD!!*

You really have to understand the layout of the backyard to realize just how perfect it was for capturing the BLACK CAT. O.K., so when you come to the walkway that leads to the back of the house, you go downhill to the bottom of the back stairs.

Up you go onto several stairs, where you land on a concrete porch that is quite high off the ground and very large. If instead you continue down the walkway, you are in the back yard, and you can see how extremely high the porch is. It was made with huge rocks that were cemented together to form the patio walls. Most of it had ivy vines growing up it.

Now, back at the top of the stairs on the porch, you walk to a screen door, walk up two stairs, and then there is the big back door. From there, you step into the kitchen and the main floor of the house. All the kids loved hanging out on the back porch because it was up high, and you could look down to the back yard and see the trees and everything going on!

And so, the day had come. Ellen and Karen S. wanted to see us capture the BLACK CAT and my Dad said it was O.K., if we were all extremely quiet. We had to get everything set up; with me dangling the tuna can from the back porch down near the ground of the back yard, my Dad with the trash can ready, and the rest of the gang hiding down low with me.

We had to make sure the BLACK CAT would not see or hear us. We waited until he came creeping close to the back wall of the porch to see if he would fall for this trick. My Dad hid behind the corner of the high stone wall down below.

It took a few minutes and in between that time it was hard not to laugh at the BLACK CAT coming closer...He was so dumb to fall for this trick. And you know, once one of you laughs, the rest of you start to laugh and then well, you know... That's when my Dad got mad and yelled up to us to be quiet (loud whispering.) *WE COULD NOT MESS THIS UP,* because we needed **THE PLAN** to work. We had to save Peanuts!

Up on the porch, I lowered the can of tuna very slowly in front of the trash can. My Dad waited until the BLACK CAT was right in front of it. He crept over very slowly and scooped up the BLACK CAT into the trash can. Then he ran to put it into the trunk of the car in the garage.

It was amazing but **THE PLAN** worked! Off we went, driving to Canton. We all heard the BLACK CAT crying and banging around in the trunk so the sooner we got to Canton the better!

Doesn't it always seem to take forever when you are going somewhere important? We finally went around the Rt. 128 rotary and took the exit where the sign said Canton Street. My Mom said, "Tom, this looks like a good neighborhood with some woods and yards the BLACK CAT could explore.

People will feed him when he comes around here for sure." Then my Dad said, "Yup, I think this is a good spot too", and he pulled the car over to the side of the road.

He opened the trunk and out leapt the

BLACK CAT who ran so fast, we could hardly see where he went. My Dad turned the car around to make our way back home. It was getting dark now and I asked quietly, "Hey Dad, do you think the BLACK CAT will be gone for good? Do you think he will forget about Peanuts now?", and my Dad said, "Don't worry about a thing, Peg. He is far away now. Everything will be fine for Peanuts to play outside."

Now you might think that this is where the story ends, but you would be sadly mistaken. Our family was determined to keep the BLACK CAT away from Peanuts. We still felt like we had to watch out for the BLACK CAT even though we knew Peanuts was safe. I know that sounds crazy but, that BLACK CAT really scared our family and the whole neighborhood, too...

CHAPTER EIGHT

The Black Cat Returns AGAIN!

The hazy, lazy days of summer went on and we kids were having a blast! We went over to each other's houses for dinner and sometimes we slept overnight at the Stack's house, or they stayed at our house. Most of the time it was Ellen that stayed over. Karen S.

usually did not want to be away from home.

It was fun to see how the other families in the neighborhood had different ways of serving dinner and had different foods they ate. Since the Stacks were such a large family, I was grateful that they would even *think* of letting me stay for dinner. I would be another mouth to feed! But it was no bother for them, and I felt special sitting at their large dining room table.

The Stack's house was set up really differently than ours. They had a huge front porch and you had to walk up a few stairs to get to the front door. We always called for Ellen and Karen S. at the back door which was down at the beginning of their driveway.

When you walked in through the front door, you were in the living room which had a big stairway that wound around a corner to the upstairs bedrooms. I don't know how they all fit into the three bedrooms, but they managed.

Then, from the living room, you walked into the dining room. They had a huge dining room table and chairs and a big hutch against the wall. They also had a built in China cabinet which always caught my attention. They had cool collectible items in there like special China and silverware! I loved how everything was different from our house!

I used to eat supper at the Carey kids house, too! Ya, I know, I guess I was kind of a good guest or something! It was so fun at their house because they had different foods I got to try.

They had Irish Soda bread with every dinner and potatoes that were so delicious! I loved chatting with them, and hearing Pat and Una talk with their Irish accents!

We were outside playing, a few weeks later when Karen came running into Eddie Pearson's yard. She was gasping for air when she said to me and Ellen, "You guys, you are not going to believe this! I just saw the BLACK CAT in your backyard, Ellen!"

We both jumped up to look over towards her back yard. And there he was. My eyes grew wide when Ellen yelled out, *"I CAN'T BELIEVE THIS! I THOUGHT YOU DROVE THAT BLACK CAT OVER TO CANTON AND DROPPED HIM OFF??"* I yelled, *"OF COURSE WE DID! HOW COULD HE MAKE HIS WAY ALL THE WAY OVER FROM CANTON TO HERE? MY DAD SAID NO WAY THAT IT WAS IMPOSSIBLE, BUT HERE HE IS!!!"* Karen said, "Peggy, we have to tell Dad at dinner. What are we going to do? How are we going to get this cat away from Peanuts again??" she cried!

My head was spinning with all kinds of thoughts! I stared into space as I pictured the BLACK CAT crossing the highway and going through traffic, like we did when we dropped him off. I kept thinking about how it was just incredible he could find his way back. All that way from Canton!

Just then, we could hear my Mom yelling, "*KAREN, PEGGY, TIME FOR DINNER!*" My Mom was calling us to come home so Ellen ran off to her house and yelled as she was running, ***"GOOD LUCK, YOU GUYS!"*** Back then, Moms would call out loud into the back yards to get us to come home from playing outside.

And then it happened. It was a couple of weeks later, in the middle of the night when I was awakened by a scream outside that sounded like cats fighting. At first, I thought I was dreaming, but then as I sat up, I heard it again outside our open window.

I jumped off the bed, raced to my parent's room, flung open their door, and yelled, "*MOM, DAD, THERE ARE CATS SCREAMING IN THE YARD, IS PEANUTS SAFE!??*"

Karen had jumped up and followed me, but I was unaware of anything except hunting for Peanuts. I was praying that he was not in this cat fight. He should have been in the back entryway of the house.

Did he get out? Did we forget to lock the back screen door? These were the thoughts that were racing through my mind as Karen, and I ran like the wind!

Usually, Peanuts slept in the entryway between the back door and the screen door that led to the back porch. It had a latch we closed every night to keep Peanuts safe. But it was half open! I ran down the back porch stairs with Karen following me, when we saw a sight, I will never forget. The BLACK CAT

had Peanuts pinned to the ground and was growling and biting Peanut's neck!! I screamed out loud, as my parents rounded the corner and my Dad yelled, **"GET AWAY! GET AWAY FROM**

PEANUTS!" at the BLACK CAT to get off! As the BLACK CAT ran, we picked Peanuts up as he cried from pain and brought him in the house.

It seemed like many days went by; all of us were taking turns feeding Peanuts milk from an eye dropper. This was the best way we could nurse him back to health. We didn't know if he would survive this attack and all anyone could think about was *REVENGE!*

CHAPTER NINE

CAPTURE PLAN Number 2

I was anxious to hear what kind of **PLAN** my father would cook up this time. We had to get rid of the BLACK CAT for the last time. Karen and I went out to play and thankfully the Stack's kids were already outside. I always felt better when I talked to Ellen about stuff.

Ellen asked us what our parents said about the whole BLACK CAT situation. I told them my Dad was trying to come up with a **PLAN**, but we probably wouldn't know until tomorrow. So, we played until dark and ran home.

The next morning my Dad rushed off to work as usual and it was not until that night that he told us **THE PLAN**. It was the same **PLAN** as before, only this time we were going to drive even further away, to the Wharf on Atlantic Avenue in Boston. Think of how well fed he would be there! We weren't at all sure the BLACK CAT would fall for this trap **_again,_** but my Dad could not think of anything else to do.

"This is going to be a tricky capture," my Dad said. He then told us that he would put the trash can in the trunk of the car and we would drive to Boston Harbor! He had a friend who was a Chef! Chef Bernie worked in a restaurant at the Harbor and already owned a couple of cats.

The restaurant was called "Anthony's Pier 5". Chef Bernie said he wouldn't mind having another cat to feed because they kept away the mice.

So, Karen was supposed to be on the lookout again, but remember that she was younger and could sometimes not pay attention. I think my Dad gave her that job because he wanted her to be a part of **THE PLAN...** but I am sure he figured the whole neighborhood would be on alert.

So now we waited... We all knew it was only a matter of time before the BLACK CAT would come strolling through our yard. Sure enough, it was about a week before *he was back in the neighborhood!* Karen spotted that *BLACK CAT ,RIGHT IN OUR OWN*

BACK YARD, AGAIN!

Now, we really could not mess this up, because the BLACK CAT would never fall for this trick again and again. (I mean, he was dumb but not that dumb, I don't think.)

So, like a well-oiled machine, we all did our parts and we captured him. *I know, we couldn't believe it either!* Then my dad put the trash can into the trunk of the car and we all took off to Boston.

By now it was dark out and I already told you where we would end up, but we had no idea how *LONG* it was going to take to get there! So, while we were driving there, my Mom decided to tell us a story about her and her best friend Kay. She figured it would help keep us all calm and it would pass the time faster.

My Mom began, "O.K. kids, listen to this story. In the early sixties everyone was obsessed with Elizabeth Taylor. She was gorgeous! We tried to copy her low-cut dresses, but that really didn't work for us. So, we copied her make-up, and we even bought her awfully expensive cologne. It was called something about diamonds, of course.

One winter night in Boston, after attending an evening performance of **<u>Hamlet,</u>** starring Richard Burton (Liz Taylor's husband), we decided to wait for him at the backstage door. Kay was sure he would be leaving by that exit from the theater.... and she was right!! A lot of other people guessed the same thing!

Who would think that a big star like him would pick such an obvious way to leave the theater, but that was Richard Burton, no muss, no fuss.

Somehow, Kay knew that his beloved Liz would be waiting in a cab at the very same location! And so, we stood there like frozen mummies in the screaming crowd. For once, we were speechless! Everyone was yelling, "*We Love you, Richard! We Love you, Liz!*" Elizabeth jumped out of the cab. Of course, she was accompanied by a couple of body guards. She was incredibly beautiful, and Richard looked like the handsome knight from Camelot!

As predicted, she scurried to meet Richard with big hugs and kisses. The crowd went nuts! We could not believe it! They were amazing. They actually stopped to sign autographs and even chatted a little bit, here and there."

Just then, Amy jumped up and asked sleepily, "Hey, Mom, did Richard kiss you, too?" My Mom laughed and answered, "Not that time, Amy-Lou, not that time!"

My Mom went on with her story. "We didn't have a moment to lose, and without missing a beat, we hailed a cab and followed their cab to an incredibly famous restaurant down at the waterfront! Guess what it was called? Anthony's Pier 5! The same restaurant we are bringing the BLACK CAT to!

Everyone knows how to get there.

Just after we entered the place, we thought we were all set.... this big tough guy near the door said very loudly, ***"This is a private party, LADIES."*** ("I hate it when people call us that. They are just trying to put us down and it's definitely not a compliment.") Karen, who was noticeably quiet up until now said, "Yeah, Ma. I hate that, too." We all broke up laughing.

My Mom continued, "We moved a little slowly, and a little closer to the movie stars. But then, the tough guy piped up *AGAIN*, a little more politely this time, "You will have to leave right now, please." We nodded okay.

But, what the heck! We got to see our favorite movie stars, we saw a great play, we had an exciting time, and I even got a wink from Richard Burton! (Kay said that he wasn't really winking at me. He was just squinting from the camera lights.) Poor thing, She was so Jealous!

CHAPTER TEN

A New Home for the Black Cat

Just then, my dad stopped the car. The smell of fish swirled into our car windows. My Mom said "Okay, now I feel better. This is a safe place for the BLACK CAT." She reassured us kids that this was, in fact, a very safe place for that "troubled hungry cat."

I will let my mom finish this part of the story because she tells it so well! My Mom said, "A few minutes later, Tom headed back to the trunk of the station wagon and waited for Bernie to give him the GO sign!"

My Mom continued, "Tom kept pointing to the car while we all tried to remain quiet. We were afraid that Bernie would say 'No Go!' It seemed like he had enough cats already. We could see at least three more chubby little ones, prancing around his feet.

Bernie stood in the kitchen doorway, under the lights, and with a big smile and a nod, he sent Tom the thumbs up! Tom opened the trunk, took off the trash can cover, and flew out this great big ball of black fur... He literally "flew" out of that dark, jail house of a trash can to what every cat dreams about...Fish, Fish, and more Fish. He obviously smelled the fish scraps waiting for him.

Believe it or not, he even allowed Bernie to bend down and pat him on the head! The BLACK CAT didn't even growl or hiss at Bernie! It was clear he had found a new place and a job (hunting down mice) where he belonged.

We found out later that he really WAS a great mouser. No trouble or fights with other cats either, *REALLY????* Peg summed it all up when she asked, 'Mom, do you think that the BLACK CAT found himself a REAL home?' I answered, 'Yes, big girl, he certainly did!'

Poor Amy was so sleepy and scared. She thought that we were going to leave her there, too! She said she dreamed that 'Bernie was making me wash dishes for the restaurant every night... and the BLACK CAT laughed and laughed and ran circles all around me... I really don't rike him ...*LETS GO HOME*!'

And so, the sunny days of summer

passed, one by one, as the days turned into weeks, and soon we noticed that there was no BLACK CAT in sight. It was a huge relief to know that Peanuts could live a life of freedom again. He could spend time with the whole neighborhood, take walks dressed up in the baby carriage, and sleep safe in the breezeway of the back porch.

What a life!

Karen and I went to bed that night whispering back and forth about all that had happened. It was quite an adventure! She said, "Peggy, that was a really long ride, wasn't it?"and I whispered back, "Yeah, it really was. I was trying hard not to fall asleep!", and then Karen said, "I know, me too! I hope that the BLACK CAT is so happy eating all that fish with the other cats, that he won't even remember Peanuts, right Peg?" and I said, "Oh my gosh, I know! Let's pray that he never thinks of Peanuts again!"

And just then, I yawned as I looked over at Karen and she was fast asleep. So, I rolled over, closed my eyes, and began drifting off to sleep thinking about how tomorrow we would have to tell all the kids in the neighborhood

what had happened; Ellen, Karen S.,
Ellen C., LeAnn, MaryAnn, Kathleen,
Mary-Clare .... Sigh.... snore....

THE END

ABOUT THE BOOK

I thought you might like to know what the Oakdale kids look like as adults now! This picture was from a reunion held at the Tahiti Restaurant in Dedham. Here they are from left around the table: Mary Carty (Stephen Carty's wife), Stephen Carty, John Carty, My Mom, Karen Sherbs, Tim Sullivan, my sister Amy, MaryAnn Carty, Kathleen Sullivan and Ellen Carty.

Another photo taken at my sister Karen's Memorial Service. From left to right: My sis Amy, Kathleen Sullivan, Karen's work friend, LeAnn McComb Tibets, another work friend and Mary-Clare Sullivan.

<u>Pat and Una Carty</u>

This book is the first in a series called **"It Happened in Dedham".** The first book is called *"Nobody Likes a Tattletale"* by my sister Amy MacMannis- Freeland and our mom, Mary Parker. I think you will find both books very enjoyable and there will be more to come! We would welcome any feedback you have!!

Please send your thoughts to:

pegoneill54@gmail.com

It Happened in Dedham